Black Cat Café
Dinner Club
Cookbook

Antony Daou

Supporting Relay for life.

4/14/13

First published in 2013 in the United States
under the **BlackCat Imprint**,
a division of

Black Cat

Black Cat Ventures,
195 Main Street, Sharon Springs, NY 13459

First Edition

ISBN-13: 978-0615768021
ISBN-10: 0615768024

Black Cat

Black Cat Café Dinner Club Cookbook

*a compilation of menus and recipes
from the dinner & cooking club
at Sharon Springs' remarkable Café*

Black Cat

Black Cat Ventures LLC
195 Main Street
Sharon Springs
New York 13459

Visit the website ...

www.blackcat-ny.com

View products for sale ...

www.blackcat-alog.com

Foreword

This cookbook is the story of the dinners and classes we shared with our Dinner Club members. Our first cookbook, **Black Cat's Cooking Class Cookbook** published in 2009 has met with surprising success and continues to sell steadily at the Café and online --without any advertising or promotion at all.

And yes, more favorites that we serve at the Café are revealed for the first time.

By popular demand, at both the dinners and from people who bought our first cookbook, there are a lot of Mediterranean and especially Lebanese dishes.

In 2010, we expanded the Café to add a second floor, with a full demonstration kitchen for cooking classes and dinners. Valentine's Day 2013 marks our third anniversary in this wonderful new space.

In this beautiful space, with block-press printed wallpaper from Adelphi Paper Hangings, hundreds of classic cookbooks, comfortable furniture, even a restored 1932 Magic Chef stove (no, we don't use it!) ... we've had dozens of classes and memorable events, including Farmer John's surprise birthday party filmed for **The Fabulous Beekman Boys** reality TV show.

I had the idea for a dinner club in January 2010 when we had 2 consecutive cooking classes cancelled due to poor attendance. So I decided to simply make dinner and told a few friends and Café regulars. 25 people showed up that first night. This just might work, I thought. Lower cost and less investment –after all, a cooking class is hard work, both for the instructor and the attendees. Dinner with like-minded people who enjoy good food and good company on a cold Winter's night in upstate NY! A much cozier concept. And so, I started to spread the word both at the Café and on Facebook.

The result was several months of great fun, and delicious dinners. We had a blast! So, we did it again the next winter. Then in 2012 we introduced "Dinner Classes" which are more like demonstration classes where I cooked and explained the dishes and we had dinner together.

Here are the recipes from those dinners and classes. I hope you enjoy them as much as we all did.

Tony Daou
Sharon Springs, February, 2013

Dedications

This cookbook is dedicated to all our wonderful club members, and to our musicians, who were such a big part of making the club such a blast!

To our incredible Black Cat team, who supported and served (and loved the food too!) and especially Caroline Chiuminato, who assisted with the classes and proofing and editing.

It is dedicated to my ex-wife Vanessa Daou, with whom I started the Café and cooking classes. An extremely talented baker and cook, and a wonderful partner in dozens and dozens of cooking classes, and a continuing inspiration to me when I started doing them on my own. And to my mother, Suzanna Daou, who helped inspire my early love of cooking and food and entertaining.

Finally, and especially to my amazing children, Sebastian, Nicholas, Isabella, Adrian and Julian.

Tony Daou
Sharon Springs, February 2013

Chuck and Jeff

How this Cookbook is Organized

Because of the two different kinds of dinners, club dinners and classes, this cookbook is organized by recipes.

It is divided into different parts of the meal, i.e. starters, soups, entrees, desserts etc. Also many of the dinners had cross-over menus. However in the commentary you'll find suggestions for accompanying sides and menus.

In several cases we'd have a class on how to make a dish from scratch, like duck leg confit, and then a dinner where we only served the finished dish. You'll find those next to each other.

There are a few recipes from our first cookbook (some have been adapted slightly,) because they were so popular at the Dinner Clubs.

Finally, I strongly emphasize the use of seasonal and local produce and meats – after all the most important part of good cooking is great ingredients.

PRIVATE PARTY

MEMBERS & GUESTS ONLY

Black Cat Cooking & Dinner Club
Join the Club!
RSVP 518.284.2575 or email
info@BlackCat-NY.com

Table of Contents

Introduction

A dinner club, also often known as a supper club, is something like a "guestaurant," a hybrid between the experiences of being a guest at a dinner party compared to a restaurant - basically a restaurant in the cook's dining room.

And they have quite a history.

In fact they were an interesting part of the development of the modern restaurant and nightclubs we know today.

The original supper club was a gathering where people met and enjoyed an evening of dining (often a "surf and turf" meal), drinks and usually live musical entertainment in a semi-formal setting. These clubs may have even helped to launch many musical careers, local legends have it that Tommy Dorsey, Gene Krupa, Glenn Miller played supper clubs. Supper clubs are even reputed to have pioneered the "doggie bag," probably because the meals were so big.

As an aside, isn't it appropriate that just as the original cabaret began in Paris with Rodolphe Salis' events at Le Chat Noir at the end of the 19th century, a supper club should find success at our tiny Black Cat Café in the 21st?

What is a Dinner or Supper Club?

The resurgence of interest in supper clubs comes from a longing to recapture a period when people made time for each other and gathered with friends who shared a mutual passion for food. We're looking for deeper connection with others, in a way that is more affordable than an expensive night "out on the town."

Here's the story of how supper clubs started.

Although dinner and supper club are interchangeable terms today, they began as supper clubs that first appeared in America's Upper Midwest: Wisconsin, Minnesota, and Michigan. Typically located on the edge of small towns in rural areas, they were traditionally thought of as a "destination" where patrons would go to spend a whole evening, from cocktail hour to nightclub style entertainment and of course, dinner. The atmosphere was casual and relaxed; most people knew each other.

According to the Wisconsin Historical Society, the development of America's highway systems and the rise of recreational auto travel had a huge impact on the growth of supper clubs. In their heyday, most were located in resort areas or near major roadways.

Supper clubs generally had straightforward menus with limited offerings featuring

"American" cuisine like prime rib, steaks, chicken, and fish. For example, an "all you can eat" Friday fish fry was particularly common at supper clubs in Wisconsin.

From humble beginnings the idea began to spread.

According to most sources, the "first" supper club outside the Midwest was established in Beverly Hills, California, by Milwaukee native Lawrence Frank. As the concept spread, they became very popular during the 1930s and 1940s – many had previously achieved notoriety as Prohibition roadhouses.

The Country Cousin

Dennis Getto, late food critic for the *Milwaukee Journal Sentinel*, once tried to fashion a working definition of the supper club for his readers. But he said that a precise definition eluded him despite thousands of miles and hundreds of dinners of "research." He did offer some very useful generalities.

He described the supper club as a "country cousin" of the urban nightclub: the main difference being that they usually outlasted their fickle, capricious city counterparts. He noted that their relaxed mood made them a destination for an entire evening of food, socializing and entertainment.

Wisconsin's Historical Society attributes the spread of the supper club to a native son, but not on native soil. Lawrence Frank from

Milwaukee established the first supper club in Beverly Hills. His simple menus included prime rib, potatoes, cooked vegetables and Yorkshire pudding. As a fascinating aside, he has been credited with the concept of a "doggie bag" for take-away leftovers from the often enormous meals.

But "supper club" has taken on new meanings, too. Like a book club, contemporary foodies often gather informally to share culinary skills in a "supper club" held in a home kitchen. More recently the term has been used by many a chef-of-the-moment to describe a prix-fixe, invitation-only sampling of new menus at exclusive or impromptu locations.

When it comes to dinner clubs, America's Midwest supper clubs have more in common with Europe than we might imagine. *supperclub*, started in Amsterdam in 1999 as an international nightclub chain that offered an aura of exclusivity to its clientele. Billed as a "free state of sensual experiences," *supperclub* is known for dining bedside with live theatrical performances between courses (wryly dubbed "intercourses.") Dinner in bed --and don't worry about the crumbs!

The concept spread across the Atlantic and south of the border.

Supper clubs in London took the cabaret concept of the American 1930s and 1940s bringing the ambience of the underground New York jazz club to the British entertainment scene, where people could enjoy a dinner with less formality, while enjoying live music. As they spread they became vital parts of social networks in both rural and urban communities.

Traditional supper club menus began with standard American fare, but there was a concerted drive to give the food and wine a British twist. Some clubs were purely informal dining societies. Others added live music. Both have largely been replaced by modern nightclubs.

Today the dinner club is enjoying a revival with a somewhat different purpose - generally a small underground gathering (often with changing premises only revealed to the guests when they bought a ticket) where guests eat from a restricted or set menu and fraternize with other guests who they may not know, but who have similar food interests.

In the UK "Underground Restaurants" and "Supper Clubs" have started to blossom, with reviews in prominent newspapers like *The Times* and *The Guardian*. Mainly concentrated in London, and some other big cities, they are advertised by word of mouth or on social media networks. They have grown so much in popularity that you can now find social networks dedicated solely to underground dining.

In Latin countries, "Supper Club" typically denotes underground restaurants, where they are known as either a *paladar* or a *restaurante de puertas cerradas* (locked door restaurant). While sometimes not even licensed restaurants, they are built into the culture, and often have higher standards than many licensed establishments.

The underground restaurant.

The attraction of the underground restaurant for the customer is the ability to sample new food at low cost outside the traditional restaurant experience, which can be expensive and disappointing— underground restaurants have been described as "anti-restaurants."

For the host, the benefit is to experiment with cooking without being required to invest in a full-time restaurant. "It's literally like playing restaurant," one host told the San Francisco Chronicle, "You can create the event, and then it's over."

There's even a recent cookbook *Friends at the Table: The Ultimate Supper Club Cookbook*, 2011 by Debi Shawcross, which sets about to tell you everything you need to know to form your own supper club.

Willis Miller, the late historian and publisher, was reported by a friend as having said on their way to a supper club:

"Well, really, Brenda, if you have good food and serve it in a tent, people will come."

I couldn't say it better.

Playing for their Supper, literally

Many wonderful local musicians and groups joined us for many of the dinners – including in no particular order: Jeff Syman, Chuck Matteson, Rich Mollin, Art Dudley, David Gibson, *Expectations*, Chris DeVille, Sandy Peevers, Jim Faliveno, Richard Saba, Erik House, Carl Waldman, *Diane Ducey and the Measured Mile*, John Resch, and several sit-ins. Their reward was of course their dinner, but even more so the pleasure and atmosphere they brought to these memorable evenings. I apologize if I have forgotten anybody. But one thing they all had in common was that they had to perform our theme song -- and look at me with straight faces as they performed it ...

Our theme song ...

Hey Good Lookin'

Hey, hey, good lookin',
Whatcha got cookin'?
How's about cookin' somethin' up with me?
Hey, sweet baby,
Don't you think maybe
We could find us a brand new recipe?
I got a hot-rod Ford and a two-dollar bill
And I know a spot right over the hill.
There's soda pop and the dancin's free,
So if you wanna have fun come along with
me.
Hey, good lookin',
Whatcha got cookin'?
How's about cookin' somethin' up with me?

I'm free and ready,
So we can go steady.
How's about savin' all your time for me?
No more lookin',
I know I've been tooken [sic].
How's about keepin' steady company?

I'm gonna throw my date-book over the
fence
And find me one for five or ten cents.
I'll keep it 'til it's covered with age
'Cause I'm writin' your name down on every
page.
Hey, good lookin',
Whatcha got cookin'?
How's about cookin' somethin' up with me?

Appetizers

Lebanese Garlic Wings

Jawaneh b'Toum

12 chicken wings
8 garlic cloves, crushed
2 tbsp olive oil
1 lemon, juiced
¼ tsp cinnamon
½ tsp ground allspice
salt and pepper to taste
pinch of cayenne pepper

Rinse the chicken wings in cold water and pat dry. Make marinade with remaining ingredients in a large bowl, add wings and coat well. Marinate in the refrigerator overnight or at room temperature for at least 2 hours.

Bake in a 400ºF oven for about 12 minutes on a side, until crispy and even a little dark. Serve with garlic dip, below.

Serves 4-6.

Lebanese Garlic Dip for Chicken

8-12 garlic cloves, peeled
½ tsp sea salt
½ lemon, juiced
4 tbsp olive oil
1 medium boiled potato, mashed

Typically served on the side with Roast Chicken, it is also a perfect accompaniment to Lebanese Garlic Chicken Wings.

Place garlic and salt in a mortar and lb. to a paste. Place in a mixing bowl and lemon juice, then slowly whisk in olive oil until creamy. To adjust "garlicky" taste and extend, mix in the mashed potato, and whisk until you get a smooth, creamy consistency. Adjust flavors to taste.

Catalan Tomato and Garlic Toasts

Pa amb Tomàquet

bread slices or rounds
extra-virgin olive oil
salt and pepper to taste
1 very ripe tomato
4 garlic cloves, mashed

This distinctive Catalan tapa is very simple: rustic, day-old bread, vine-ripe tomato, some pungent extra virgin olive oil and sea salt makes *pa amb tomàquet,* Catalonia's favorite breakfast, tapa, lunch and late-night supper

Toast the bread on both sides. Spread the mashed garlic on the top side. Cut the tomato in half and rub the cut side into the bread until it is well moistened with pulp. Repeat on the other side.

Drizzle the top side generously with olive oil and sprinkle with sea salt. You can accompany pa amb tomàquet with anchovies or with some sliced *jamón* (ham) or *salchichón* (cured pork sausage) or just enjoy as a starter.

Artisan Bread, Olives & Olive Oil

There's nothing like really good hot bread with scrumptious olives and excellent olive oil to start a meal!

Simply slice and toast 2 or 3 kinds of bread (the ends work great too!) and arrange in a circle on a plate with a little ramekin of olive oil surrounded by our favorite olives.

No-knead Bread

Jim Lahey of Sullivan Street Bakery in NY started a rage of bread making with Mark Bittman of the NY Times' "No-Knead Bread" article on November 8, 2006. It was the most shared New York Times article that month, and one of the most popular of all time. Countless follow-up articles and versions by numerous bakers have since appeared.

We've been baking it at the Café ever since and have modified it a little for our own versions.

Basic Recipe, White Boule

3 cups white bread (high-gluten) flour, more for dusting
¼ tsp instant yeast
1 5/8 cups tepid water
1¼ tsp salt
cornmeal or wheat bran as needed for dusting
4 quart oven-proof pot

In a large bowl, combine flour, yeast and salt. Add the water, and stir until blended; dough will be shaggy and sticky. Cover bowl with plastic wrap. Let dough rest for 12-18 hours at room temperature.

Dough is ready when its surface is dotted with bubbles. Lightly flour a work surface and place dough on it; sprinkle it with a little more flour and fold it over on itself once or twice. Using just enough flour to keep dough from sticking to work surface or to your fingers, gently and quickly shape dough into a ball. Generously coat a cotton towel (not terry cloth) with flour, wheat bran or cornmeal; put dough seam side down on towel and dust with more flour, bran or cornmeal. Cover with another cotton towel and let rise for about 2 hours.

When it is ready, dough will be more than double in size and will not readily spring back when poked with a finger.

About a half-hour before dough is ready, heat oven to 500°F. Put a 6-quart heavy covered pot (cast iron, enamel, Pyrex or ceramic) in oven as it heats. When dough is ready, carefully remove pot from oven. Slide your hand under towel and turn dough over into pot, seam side up; it may look like a mess, but that is fine.

Shake pan once or twice if dough is unevenly distributed; it will straighten out as it bakes. Cover with lid and bake 30 minutes, then remove lid and bake another 15 to 30 minutes, until loaf is beautifully browned. Cool on a rack. Will keep several days and freezes beautifully.

Black Cat's Variations

At the Café we make several popular variations, but we make 2 or 3 dozen loaves at a time. While testing these versions, we found that quantity does make a difference, so these are adapted for home use, two loaves at a time. Use a 6-qt. cast-iron covered pot and cornmeal or wheat bran for dusting.

Black Cat Café's Honey Rye
5 ½ cups high-gluten white flour
1 ½ cups rye flour
¾ tsp instant yeast
4 ½ cups tepid water
4 tsp salt
2 tbsp caraway seeds
a good splash of honey

Black Cat Café's Cinnamon Raisin
7 ½ cups high-gluten white flour
½ tsp instant yeast
4 ½ cups tepid water
3 tsp salt
4 cups raisins
1 ½ tbsp cinnamon

Black Cat Café's Whole Wheat
5 cups white bread high-gluten flour
3 cups wheat bread flour
½ tsp instant yeast
4 ½ cups tepid water
4 tsp salt

Labneh, Lebanese Yogurt

Just like hummus, this is a wonderful appetizer as part of a typical Lebanese meza. It is also often served at breakfast. Labneh is now available in many premium and ethnic supermarkets, but an easy and ubiquitous replacement is 2% Greek Yogurt, like Fage or Chobani.

Serve sprinkled with za'atar or garnished with fresh mint leaves and drizzled with a little extra-virgin olive oil, with toasted pita bread triangles and some nice olives.

Making Labneh at Home

1 quart of plain yogurt (full fat yields a creamier texture of cheese)
Thick cheesecloth and 6-8 clothespins
2 stainless steel or glass bowls
String or very thick rubber band

Pour yogurt into a large bowl and stir until just smooth. Take the cheesecloth and fold into several layers. Place it in the 2nd bowl so that it is lying flat against the bottom with the ends up and over the sides of the bowl. Use clothespins to pin cheesecloth securely to edges of the bowl.

Transfer yogurt into the bowl with the cheesecloth, then gather up the ends and remove the clothespins one at a time to end up with a cheesecloth "sack" containing the yogurt. Tie top securely with string or wrap with the rubber band making sure to leave a loop from which to hang it. (You could also make a bag of thick cheesecloth with a drawstring.)

Hang the sack with the yogurt from a cabinet knob or handle and place a bowl underneath to catch the whey that will drain out of the yogurt. Let drain for 8 to 12 hours. The longer the yogurt drains, the thicker the labneh will be. Overnight is a common rule of thumb.

Remove the sack and open it up, over a bowl and scrape the rest of the labneh off with a wooden spoon. Discard the whey or liquid that has drained out of the yogurt. Store in the refrigerator. It should keep for approximately one week.

One cup of yogurt yields about 1/3 to 1/2 cup of labneh.

Lebanese Hummus

4 cups cooked chick peas
1 scant cup sesame tahini
1 tsp salt
4 lemons, juiced
6 garlic cloves, crushed
¼ cup extra-virgin olive oil
a dash of sweet paprika
1 tbsp toasted pine nuts

The night before soak chick peas in 3 times their volume of water. (Optional: add a little baking soda to soften them & reduce cooking time.) The chick peas should double in size.

Rinse soaked (or canned) chick peas under cold water. Place in a saucepan over high heat and cover well with cold water. Bring to a boil. Reduce heat, cover and cook for about 1½ hours or until very tender. Drain, reserving some of the cooking water.

In a food processor or blender, blend chickpeas to a smooth puree, add tahini, salt to taste and blend well. Pour in half the lemon juice gradually, and taste. Add garlic and mix again. If too thick – it should be soft and creamy but not runny -- add some of the reserved cooking water.

Serve in small shallow bowls. Make a dip in the center for some olive oil, garnish with paprika and a few whole chickpeas or pine nuts. Serve with pita slices.

Golden-fried Cauliflower Florets

Based on a Lebanese recipe, here's a great way to make local Cauliflower delectable. Serve with Tahini dip for a Lebanese flavor.

1-2 cauliflowers cut in medium-sized florets
salt to taste
vegetable oil for frying
2 tsp pomegranate molasses (*Ribb al-Rumman*)

Blanch the florets for 2-3 minutes, or until half-cooked, then drain and dry on paper towels.

Heat enough oil in a skillet or pot to deep fry the cauliflower. Oil should be hot enough that when you test with a floret the oil should bubble around it. Carefully fry (in batches if necessary) until golden all over, but not brown. Remove with slotted spoon and drain on paper towels.

Serve at room temperature with a side dish of yogurt or with a drizzle of Pomegranate Molasses (a great Lebanese favorite of ours, now available in most specialty and organic food stores.)

Eggplant Wedges with Walnuts & Garlic

This strongly flavored version of a common Turkish meza dish supposedly originates in Georgia (the country.) It is traditionally served cold, and can be made a day ahead.

2 lbs. eggplant
extra virgin olive oil
3 tbsp white wine vinegar
salt to taste
6 garlic cloves, crushed
½ cup walnuts
¼ cup chopped flat-leaf parsley

Cut eggplants lengthwise into slices about a quarter of an inch thick. Place on an oven tray and brush both sides generously with olive oil. Cook in a very hot oven (475°F) for about 20 minutes or until lightly browned and soft, turning over once.

Arrange on flat serving plates, then brush with vinegar and sprinkle lightly with salt. Soften garlic in 1 tbsp of olive oil over medium heat until the aroma rises, but do not let it color. Finely chop the walnuts in a food processor and mix with the chopped parsley in a bowl. Add the garlic with another tbsp of olive oil and sprinkling of salt, mix well, and spread on the eggplant slices. Serves 8 as an appetizer.

Pan-Seared Chicken Livers

Fresh local chicken livers are one of the great unsung delicacies. My kids can easily eat a pound or even two at a sitting (well I do have 5 children!)

1 lb fresh local chicken livers (and hearts)
2 tbsp butter
1-2 tsp fine salt
2 dozen melba toasts or little crostinis
1 tsp Sel Gris
A good skillet, preferably cast-iron

Cover the bottom of a skillet with fine salt and heat over very high heat. Separate the livers with a very sharp knife and discard any veins (if any hearts cut them in half.) Once the pan is very hot, add the livers (and hearts if you have them.)

The livers should sizzle and burble (yes, burble and pop) right away otherwise your pan is not hot enough. Sear about 2-3 minutes then flip over. Add the butter in little chunks and sear another minute or two. Just before butter starts to brown, turn off heat, remove skillet and set aside.

The livers will continue to cook if you want them well-done, otherwise remove immediately (they will be medium rare) and place a liver or heart on each toast. Sprinkle with a tiny pinch of Sel Gris and serve immediately.

Potato-Leek BLAAK Cheese Tartlet

The sweet tart shells and savory filling make a wonderful combination and highlight Beekman 1802's wonderful BLAAK goat cheese.

10 pre-baked Pâte Sucrée 3" tartlet shells, (either purchased or see recipe following)
2 tbsp butter
1 medium leek, (clean, wash & pat dry)
1 ½ medium potatoes, peeled and diced
4 eggs
½ cup cream
½ cup grated Beekman BLAAK cheese
¾ tsp fresh thyme
¼ tsp each of salt & freshly-ground pepper

Preheat oven to 350°F. Bake off the tart shells (about 15-20 minutes.)

Dice leek finely, using all the white part and some of the tender green. Melt butter in a skillet over medium heat and cook till translucent. Add potato, cover pan and cook until tender, about 10 minutes. Uncover and sprinkle with thyme, salt & pepper, Give the mixture a good stir and set aside to cool. Whip together eggs & cream. Add cooled mixture and combine.

Place in the baked, cooled tart shells, filling just below the top, sprinkle the cheese on top till level with shell, and bake another 10-15 minutes until set. Serve hot or at room temperature.

Sweet Tart Dough

Pâte Sucrée Tartlet Shells

This recipe makes a terrific blind-baked tart shell to fill and bake your favorite tart, or to fill and serve as is. "Blind" baking means to pre-bake a tart or pie shell without filling. In classical French cuisine it is referred to as "cuire a blanc". You can add more sugar if you like a sweeter dough, and you may also make this recipe by hand using a pastry cutter rather than a food processor.

Makes one 10-inch tart shell or eight 3" tartlet shells.

8 tart shell molds or a 10" tart pan
½ cup (8 tbsp) cold unsalted butter
2 tbsp ice water
1 ¼ cups all-purpose flour
1 ½ tsp sugar
1 large egg yolk
Plastic Wrap

Cut the butter into small pieces, place in a bowl, and refrigerate to chill while you are setting up. Set aside a 9 or 10-inch tart pan with removable bottom. Prepare a small bowl with ice water.

Place the flour and sugar in the bowl of a food processor. Pulse several times to combine. Place the egg yolk in a small bowl and add the ice water, whisk to combine.

Add the chilled butter pieces to the food processor and pulse approximately 6 to 8 times until the mixture resembles a coarse meal. Do not over-process the dough! The butter should remain in tiny pieces.

Sprinkle the yolk/ice water mixture over the dough. Pulse several times, just until the dough holds together without being wet or sticky. Test the dough by squeezing a small amount together in the palm of your hand. If the dough still seems a bit too crumbly, add a teaspoon of ice water at a time, and pulse several times until the desired consistency is achieved.

Turn the dough out onto a large piece of plastic wrap. Grasping the ends of the plastic wrap with your hands, press the dough into a flat disc with your fists. Wrap the dough and chill for at least one hour.

Remove the dough from the refrigerator and roll into a 12-inch circle. Place the dough in the tart pan and use a fork to make holes in the bottom of the crust. Cover with plastic wrap and refrigerate for one hour, or freeze for 30 minutes.

Preheat oven to 375°F.

Remove the tart shell from the refrigerator or freezer and place a large piece of parchment paper or foil in the bottom. Smooth the foil or paper to fit snugly into the shell, then fill with pie weights (dried beans or rice may be used). Place in the oven and bake for approximately 20 minutes, or until the edges begin to brown. Remove the foil or parchment and pie weights and set them aside to cool. Place the empty shell back into the oven and continue to bake for about 10 minutes until golden brown.

For the tartlet shells, divide the dough in 8 parts and prepare each shell as above with the appropriate amount of dough.

Place the tart shell(s) on a rack and allow to cool completely before filling or baking again. If made in advance, place in an air tight container or a freezer bag and freeze.

Black Cat's Famous
Fig-Balsamic Drizzle

Gigandes beans

Gigandes beans are plump, creamy delicacies of the Mediterranean. They are grown on the mountain slopes of the Mediterranean in Greece, Italy, Spain and Lebanon.

Gigandes beans are also known as Fasolia Gigantes, or Hija or Fasoulia. These huge, sweet-tasting, creamy-white beans from the white runner bean family command high prices fresh, but with their increasing popularity are readily available dried. Today they are becoming popular in higher-end food stores usually in a simple marinade.

Serve in a simple marinade of your choice, like olive oil, vinegar, herbs and chopped red onions & peppers, over a bed of baby greens or as part of a meza or tapas meal.

Gigandes Plaki

This popular Greek dish consists of gigandes cooked in a tomato-based sauce. Although there are many variations, it usually consists of gigandes, tomatoes, onions, olive oil, parsley, and often sugar.

As with other beans, dried gigandes must be soaked overnight in plenty of cold water.

The next day the beans are boiled until tender and the rest of ingredients are added. In a cast-iron or oven proof skillet sauté all of the ingredients in the olive oil for 15-20 minutes. Bake in a 350°F oven until the top layer of the dish is slightly charred from the sugar reacting to the heat. Remove and let cool before garnishing with parsley and Greek feta, and serve with Greek bread.

Traditionally, gigandes plaki is served as part of a meze; however this hearty meze dish is filling enough to be eaten for lunch, especially during the cold fall and winter months.

Serves 4-6.

Zucchini Fritters

1 lb. zucchini, grated
1 onion, coarsely chopped
3 tbsp vegetable oil
3 large eggs
3 tbsp all-purpose flour
black pepper to taste
6 sprigs fresh mint, chopped
3 sprigs fresh dill, chopped
8 oz soft goat cheese

Based on a Turkish recipe, I've replaced the typical Feta cheese with soft goat cheese. A great way to use our wonderful local squash in the Summer.

Fry onion in the oil over medium heat until soft and very lightly browned. Add grated zucchini and sauté, stirring, until soft.

Beat the eggs with the flour until well-blended. Add pepper and herbs and mix well. Fold in the cheese, then the onions and zucchini.

Film the bottom of a non-stick pan with oil and fry a few at a time about 2 tbsp each, turning over once, until both sides are brown. Drain on paper towels and serve hot or cold. Serves 4.

Turkish Beets with Yogurt

1 lb. small beets
2 tbsp lemon juice
3-4 tbsp olive oil
1 cup plain Greek yogurt
Salt to taste
1 tbsp finely chopped mint

Wash, clean thoroughly and cut tops of beets off.

Drizzle very lightly with olive oil and roast in a 375°F oven until tender (about 1 hour.)

Let cool for a few minutes, then peel and slice in thin rounds or strips as you prefer.

Mix remaining (about 2 tbsp) olive oil with lemon juice. Add yogurt and salt and beat well, then mix with the beets.

Pour into a serving dish and garnish with mint.

Serves 4.

Fava Bean & Garlic-Lemon Mash

Fool m'Dammas

This Lebanese meza dish and peasant food is often served for breakfast or as a side. If using fresh, be sure to peel the skins off the Fava beans!

1 lb dried Fava (butterbeans) soaked overnight, or 2 cans
3 cloves garlic, crushed
½ cup olive oil
1 lemon, juiced
1 tsp salt
¼ tsp black pepper

Rinse and drain the beans and place in a large saucepan. Add water to cover well and bring to a boil. Reduce heat to simmer, and then cover. Check and add more water stirring it in, cooking until beans are tender, about 45 minutes total.

Drain the beans, mix in the remaining ingredients immediately.

Serve with toasted pita bread.

About 6-8 servings.

Rose Marie and Tony

Salads
&
Soups

Baby Green Salad, Lemon Dressing

Delectable local baby greens, vine-ripened tomatoes and fresh cucumbers make a simple but fabulous salad with this wonderful dressing. It is all about the quality of the ingredients.

1/3 cup lemon juice
2/3 cup extra-virgin olive oil
3 cloves garlic crushed
Salt & pepper to taste

Crush the garlic cloves with mortar and pestle (placing some salt in the bottom both for taste and to help the crushing.) mix all the ingredients together and adjust salt & pepper to taste. Depending on the oil and lemons you may need to adjust quantities slightly to taste. Makes 1 cup. Keeps, refrigerated, for about a week.

Pinzimonio: Showcasing Local Vegetables

1 fennel bulb
1 bunch celery
2 carrots
2 heirloom tomatoes
1 radicchio
1 bell pepper
extra-virgin olive oil
salt and pepper to taste

We have such incredible local vegetables (admittedly for a short time up here) that all on their own they make a great appetizer! This is one of the best-known Tuscan antipasti. *Pinzimonio* relies on the freshest vegetables and your best olive oil.

Simply clean and slice the best vegetables you can find in your garden or at the local farmer's markets and arrange on a platter with a small dipping bowl of your very best olive oil to which you have added sea salt and freshly ground pepper to taste.

Gorgonzola, Walnut, Apple & Fig Salad

with Black Cat's Fig Balsamic Drizzle

Baby greens, a large handful per plate
Honey Crisp or Granny Smith Apple, very
thinly sliced
Walnut halves
A good aged Gorgonzola
Black Cat's Fig-Balsamic Drizzle
*Optional: Dried Calmyrna Figs Marinated in
Balsamic Vinegar (make 2-3 days ahead)*

Arrange as below. Adjust proportions to
taste.

Marinated Cucumber Salad

2 English cucumbers
1/3 cup rice wine vinegar
1/3 cup good soy sauce
1/3 cup vegetable oil

This salad should be prepared just before serving and not too much ahead of time since the ingredients will marinate and soften the cucumbers, and you'll lose the fresh crunchiness. Use the best cucumbers you can find. Large "English" cucumbers are your best bet year-round, but of course during the season there is nothing like fresh local cucumbers.

Slice cucumbers into very thin rounds using a sharp knife or mandolin. Mix dressing, adjust to taste, then toss cucumber rounds in, coating thoroughly. Cover and chill for 15-20 minutes before serving.

Lebanese Cabbage Slaw

Salatet Malfouf

1 medium cabbage
2 garlic cloves, crushed
4 tbsp olive oil
1 lemon, juiced
salt to taste
black pepper to taste

Clean and quarter the cabbage, remove
core, then shred finely with a very sharp
knife or mandolin. Combine dressing
ingredients and mix well. Pour over salad
and toss.

Let stand 10-15 minutes then mix well
again before serving. Serve immediately.
This salad doesn't keep more than a day as
the cabbage with the lemon starts to
ferment even refrigerated, so make as
much as you need. It's so easy to make a
little more, anyway!

Moroccan Carrot Orange Salad

Makes a lovely starter for a Moroccan dinner.

1 lb carrots
1 large navel orange
1 tsp cinnamon
3 tbsp lemon juice
1 tbsp granulated sugar
1 tsp orange blossom water
pinch of salt

Clean, peel and grate the carrots. Peel and section the orange, and reserve the juice. Mix juice with the remaining ingredients. Stir in the carrots and orange segments, and then chill for at least 1 hour.

Before serving, drain partially if there is too much liquid.

Serves 4.

Purslane (Mâche) Salad

*This is the "other" Lebanese salad –
"Fattoush" -- much less well-known than
Tabbouleh, but in my opinion much more
interesting and elegant. Purslane also
known as Mâche lettuce from its French
name, or Lamb's Lettuce in this country, is
increasingly available these days.*

2 cups romaine, torn into 2-3" pieces
2 large heirloom tomatoes
2-3 small cucumbers, peeled
3 green onions, minced
15-20 mint leaves chopped
¼ cup chopped parsley
1 cup purslane leaves
2 cups toasted pita bread, broken in pieces
Classic Lemon Vinaigrette below

Cut the vegetables into bite sizes. Split
loaves of pita bread by separating the top
and bottom of the "pocket", and crisp in a
toaster or regular oven. Break with your
hands into roughly bite-size pieces.

Prepare the dressing and toss all
ingredients in a salad bowl.

Variation: Add 1-2 tbsp pomegranate
syrup to the dressing.

Lebanese Lemon Dressing

This is a variation on the delicious salad dressing that is a mainstay at the Café, using sumac and ground black pepper.

1/4 cup lemon juice
1/3 cup extra-virgin olive oil
1-2 tbsp sumac
salt to taste
pinch of pepper

Combine all ingredients in a jar with a tight-fitting lid, cover, and shake to blend.

White Bean Salad

1 lb. can of white cannelini beans
½ red onion
1 green pepper
1 very ripe tomato
1 medium cucumber
¼ cup black olives, Kalamata
4 tbsp extra-virgin olive oil
1 tbsp sherry or champagne vinegar
1 tsp salt

Rinse and drain the beans and place in a bowl. Chop vegetables into small pieces of equal size and add to bowl. Add olives.

Prepare vinaigrette to taste and add, mixing well to coat; taste for salt.

Chill for 1-2 hours before serving. Serves 6.

Roasted Beet, Walnut & Gorgonzola Salad

12 baby beets, cleaned and trimmed
6 tbsp Black Cat's Fig-balsamic Drizzle
2/3 cup chopped walnuts
10 tbsp extra-virgin olive oil
1 cup crumbled Gorgonzola cheese

Preheat oven to 400°F. Toss beets in 2 tbsp each of the oil and drizzle, then place on baking sheet and cover tightly with foil, enclosing completely.

Bake beets until fork-tender. Toast the walnuts for about 5 minutes or until they just start to brown. Let the beets cool, then peel and slice.

Whisk the remaining olive oil and the balsamic drizzle in a bowl to blend thoroughly. Pour the dressing over the warm beets.

Divide among the individual plates. Sprinkle with the cheese and toasted walnuts, and serve warm.

6-8 servings.

Soup's on

White Bean, Garlic & Sage Soup

2 tbsp butter
1 tbsp olive oil
2 shallots, chopped
6-8 sage leaves
2 (15-ounce) cans cannellini beans, drained and rinsed
4 cups low-sodium chicken broth
4-6 cloves peeled garlic, cut in halves
¼ cup heavy cream
½ tsp freshly ground black pepper
6 slices ciabatta bread
Extra-virgin olive oil, for drizzling

Place a medium soup pot over medium heat. Add butter, olive oil and shallots. Cook, stirring occasionally, until the shallots are softened, about 3-5 minutes. Add sage and beans and stir to combine.

Add the stock and bring to a simmer. Add the garlic and simmer until the garlic is softened, about 5-6 minutes. Pour the soup into a large bowl. Let cool.

Carefully ladle 1/3 to 1/2 of the soup into a blender, being sure to include all the sage and puree with the cream until smooth. Be careful to hold the top of the blender tightly, as hot liquids expand when they are blended. Pour the blended soup back into the soup pot; add salt & the pepper to taste. Keep warm, covered, over very low heat.

Place a grill pan over medium-high heat. Drizzle the slices of ciabatta bread with the olive oil. Grill the bread until warm and golden, about 3 minutes a side. Serve the soup in bowls with the grilled bread floating in it. Garnish with a fresh sage leaf or two.

Chilled Cucumber-Yogurt Soup

1 large or several small cucumbers
2 cups yogurt
2 tsp distilled white vinegar
1 tsp olive oil
2 tsp finely cut fresh mint or 1 tsp dried
½ tsp finely cut fresh dill or ¼ tsp dried
1 tsp salt

Peel cucumber and slice lengthwise into halves. Scoop out seeds by running the tip of a teaspoon down the center of each half. Discard the seeds and grate the cucumber coarsely. (Should make about 1 cup.)

In a deep bowl, stir the yogurt with a whisk until completely smooth. Gently but thoroughly beat in the grated cucumber, vinegar, olive oil, mint, dill and salt.

Taste for seasoning, adding more salt if necessary. Refrigerate the soup for at least 2 hours until thoroughly chilled. Serve in clear glass bowls and garnish with fresh mint in center.

Mulligatawny Soup

This Café and cooking class favorite is really a meal in itself. If you don't add the chicken, it is also an excellent Vegan choice. And it bears no resemblance to the Soup Nazi's version from Seinfeld!

2 tbsp olive oil
2 stalks celery, chopped
1 carrot, peeled and chopped
1 onion, peeled and chopped
1 2-3" piece fresh ginger, peeled and diced
1 chili pepper, seeded and de-veined
6 cups vegetable or chicken stock
1 ½ cup red lentils
salt and pepper to taste
1 tbsp curry powder
2/3 cup coconut milk
2 cups cooked basmati rice
1 cup shredded cooked chicken breast
½ cup tart raw apple, chopped

For garnish:
½ cup toasted coconut
¼ bunch fresh cilantro
2 ½ tbsp coconut milk
1 lime cut in 8 wedges

Sauté onion in oil over medium heat until they are translucent. Add carrot, celery, chili pepper and ginger. Stir in the curry powder to blend and cook for a minute. Pour in the water or stock, add the lentils and bring to a boil. Reduce heat and simmer for 30 minutes.

While the soup is simmering, get the rice cooked (if it isn't already); similarly with the chicken. Then shred the chicken and dice the apples. No need to peel apples.

When soup is done, add salt, pepper and more curry powder to taste, and then puree. Bring the soup back to a simmer and add the coconut milk. To serve, have big individual serving bowls at the ready. Fill each bowl halfway with soup then spoon some rice into the bowl. Next, add some chicken and a spoonful of chopped apple. Sprinkle with fresh cilantro and toasted coconut and serve with a wedge of lime.

Serves 6-8.

"Oops" Soup with Pesto

This is a modification of the Café's ever-popular Wild Rice & Tomato Soup. We started the soup one morning and realized we were out of wild rice. What to do? Well, Vanessa suggested we add white beans and serve with a dollop of pesto. It became such a big hit that it rivals the original Wild Rice and Tomato Soup in popularity.

5 tbsp olive oil
1 large onion, diced
2 carrots, diced
2 stalks celery, diced
4 cups crushed tomatoes
1 can white beans
4 or more cups vegetable or chicken stock
2 tsp salt
2 tsp black pepper
2 tbsp fresh or dried basil
pesto for garnish

Heat oil in large pot. Add onion, carrot and celery. Cook until vegetables are translucent, stirring.

Drain tomatoes, and then pour into pot with the stock. Bring to boil, cover, and reduce heat to a simmer. Add salt, pepper, sugar, and herbs.

Stir often and cook about 1 ½ hours. In the last 15 minutes, add the white beans. Garnish with a dollop of pesto.

Hearty Lebanese Bean Soup, *Makhloutah*

1/3 cup cannellini beans
½ cup whole dried chickpeas
½ tsp baking soda
¾ cup brown lentils
11 cups water
1/8 cup coarse bulgur wheat
1/8 cup white short-grain rice
½ cup + 2 tbsp olive oil
2 onions, finely chopped
1 tsp ground cinnamon
1 tsp ground cumin
2 tsp ground allspice
black pepper and salt to taste

The night before, put the beans and chickpeas to soak in 3 times their volume of water, and stir in the baking soda. Next day, wash the bulgur, rice and lentils separately in several changes of cold water, drain and set aside. Put lentils in a large saucepan. Rinse the beans and chickpeas under cold water, drain, and add to lentils. Pour in the water, cover pan and place over high heat. Bring to a boil, then reduce heat to medium and boil gently, covered for an hour, or until tender.

Fry chopped onion in the oil over medium heat until golden. Add the onions along with the rice and bulgur to the legumes when they are tender. Season with spices, and simmer for 15 minutes. Adjust seasoning and thickness to taste. Serves 4-6.

Fresh Local Garlic Soup

3 heads garlic
4 cups water
2 onions, finely chopped
2/3 cup extra-virgin olive oil
3 ½ cups chicken stock
10 fresh sage leaves
4 1/2-inch-thick slices good crusty bread
2/3 cup shredded Parmigiano Reggiano
salt and black pepper to taste

Separate cloves from each head of garlic but do not peel. Bring water to a rolling boil in a 2-quart saucepan. Drop in garlic cloves and boil 10 minutes. Drain in a sieve and peel. Return the garlic cloves to the saucepan, and add the onion, olive oil, sage, and stock. Bring to a lively bubble over medium-high heat. Partially cover and cook 5 minutes. Uncover, adjust the heat so the liquid bubbles slowly, and cook for another 5 minutes.

Croutons: Preheat broiler. While the soup is simmering, arrange the bread slices on a baking sheet. Toast under the broiler 1-2 minutes per side, or until the slices are crisp and golden. Set aside a few spoonfuls of the cheese to top the soup. Sprinkle the rest over the bread slices. Slip the baking sheet back under the broiler only a second or two, to melt the cheese but not brown it.

Finishing and Serving: Warm four soup bowls. The garlic cloves will be meltingly soft when the soup finishes cooking.

Remove all but 1 sage leaf, and puree the soup in a blender or food processor. Season to taste. Arrange the croutons in the soup dishes, and pour the puree over them. Sprinkle each serving with a few shreds of cheese, and serve immediately.

Serves 4.

Sides &
Vegetarian
Entrées

Sexy Exotic Mushrooms

with sage-cream sauce on mini toasts

1-2 lbs wild mushrooms, I prefer oysters,
but chanterelles, shiitakes, cremini, or any
combination works too
6 tbsp unsalted butter
2 garlic cloves, minced
Salt and pepper to taste
1 cup heavy cream
¼ cup chicken stock
1 bunch fresh sage leaves
16-20 toasts

Trim & stem the mushrooms. Slice the tops
off and try to keep as many as possible
whole.

In one skillet, melt half the butter then add
the mushroom tops, season with salt and
pepper and cook over moderately high
heat, stirring, until golden. Set skillet aside,
keeping warm in a 200F oven.

Mince the stems & trimmings and in
another skillet, fry the garlic and minced
mushrooms in half the butter. In the
meantime pick the sage leaves, reserving
several whole ones for garnish. Chop the
remaining sage leaves and add half to the
mushrooms. Add the stock and reduce.

Now add the cream and simmer over
moderate heat until slightly thickened,
about 5 minutes. Combine both skillets, add
the remaining chopped sage and simmer

for 2-3 more minutes.

Arrange 2 toasts on a plate, cover with mushrooms, garnish with a whole sage leaf. 8 servings or sides.

Oven-roasted Root Vegetables

The flavor of local root vegetables – the smaller and fresher the better – is a fabulous accompaniment or an appetizer. This one of those recipes where we simply select what's at hand or what appeals to us at the local Farmer's Markets. We prefer baby carrots, parsnips, beets and fingerling potatoes – but this dish varies every time.

Pre-heat oven to 375°F. Separate a head or two of garlic into cloves, but do not peel. Wash and pat dry the vegetables, then toss everything with olive oil, salt and pepper. Lay flat in a roasting pan in a single layer.

Cook about 30 minutes until tender or even a little crispy depending on your taste. The time will depend on the size and how many vegetables you choose.

Sexy Fried Mac & Cheese

So what makes it sexy? Frying it in butter. All that cheese and cream and butter for a start, and the frying in butter just makes it sumptuous and silky on the inside when you bite through the crispy outside.

Macaroni and Cheese

For topping
¾ stick unsalted butter
3 cups coarse fresh bread crumbs (from 6 slices firm white sandwich bread)
1½ cups coarsely grated extra-sharp Cheddar
½ cup grated good Swiss cheese

For macaroni and sauce
1 ½ sticks unsalted butter
6 tbsp all-purpose flour
4 cups whole milk
1 cup cream
6 cups coarsely grated extra-sharp Cheddar
1 cup grated good Swiss cheese
1 lb. elbow macaroni

Preheat oven to 400°F with rack in middle.

Topping: Melt butter, then stir together with bread crumbs and topping cheeses in a bowl until combined well.

Make sauce: Melt butter in a heavy medium saucepan over medium-low heat and stir in flour. Cook roux, stirring, 3 minutes, then whisk in milk. Bring sauce to a boil, whisking constantly, then simmer, whisking occasionally, 3 minutes. Stir in cheeses, 2 tsp salt, and 1/2 tsp pepper until smooth. Remove from heat and cover surface of sauce with wax paper.

Make Macaroni: Cook macaroni in a pasta pot of boiling salted water (2 tbsp salt for 4 quarts water) until al dente. Reserve 1 cup cooking water and drain macaroni in a colander. Stir together macaroni, reserved cooking water, and sauce in a large bowl. Transfer to 2 buttered 2-quart shallow baking dishes.

Sprinkle topping evenly over macaroni and bake until golden and bubbling, 20 to 25 minutes.

Let cool then refrigerate 3 hours or overnight to be sure the mac & cheese is firm. Cut into thick slices, about 2". Makes 16-20 servings.

Melt butter in a skillet until it starts to sizzle and carefully fry the mac on each side, about 3-4 minutes until crispy and the cheese just starts to melt out. Serve hot.

Black Cat's BLAAK & Mac

Beekman 1802 makes a wonderful semi-hard goat cheese (for more see next page.) It kicks our mac & cheese recipe up a notch and is a huge favorite at the Café. You can find canned goat milk at specialty stores and surprisingly even at Walmart.

For topping
½ stick unsalted butter
3 cups coarse fresh bread crumbs
1 ½ cups coarsely grated extra-sharp Cheddar
¼ cup grated Beekman BLAAK Cheese

For macaroni and sauce
1 lb. elbow macaroni
1 stick (8 tbsp) unsalted butter
¾ cup all-purpose flour
4 cups whole milk
¾ cup (6 oz.) goat milk
2 cups heavy cream
4 cups coarsely grated extra-sharp Cheddar
2 cups grated Swiss cheese
2 cups Beekman BLAAK cheese, shredded
½ tsp freshly ground black pepper
2 tsp salt

Make topping: Melt butter, then stir together with bread crumbs and topping cheeses in a bowl until combined well.

Make Macaroni: Cook macaroni in a pasta pot of boiling salted water (2 tbsp salt for 4 quarts water) until al dente. Drain well. Stir together macaroni, and sauce in a large bowl. Set aside.

Make sauce: Melt butter in a heavy medium saucepan over medium-low heat and stir in flour. Cook roux, stirring, 3 minutes, then whisk in milks & cream. Bring sauce to a boil, whisking constantly, then simmer, whisking occasionally, 3 more minutes. Stir in cheeses, salt, and tsp pepper until smooth. Remove from heat and combine with the drained macaroni. Keep it warm or refrigerate until ready.

Finishing: Place in ramekins of desired size, usually about 8 oz. Sprinkle topping evenly over macaroni and bake until golden and bubbling, if hot you can just put the topping on and place under a cheese-melter if you have one or a broiler.

Makes 20 servings

Beekman 1802 BLAAK is the famous artisan cheese produced from the goats at Beekman Farm in Sharon Springs. BLAAK is an Italian-style semi-hard cheese made from a 60:40 mix of raw goat and cow milk giving the cheese a mild but distinctive flavor. In keeping with traditional cheese-making practices, this rare cheese is aged for 3 months in caves and is coated with ash at each turning to promote the ripening of the wheel. The resulting edible black rind gives the cheese its name.

Drunken Blonde Fruitcake Stuffing

Inspired by a recipe from Josh Kilmer-Purcell of the Fabulous Beekman Boys

3-4 thick slices fruitcake, chopped
1 small onion, chopped
2 stalks celery chopped
½ cup Chicken or vegetable stock
3 tbsp butter
1 tbsp olive oil
1 tbsp Applejack
½ bunch Fresh Sage, chopped
Salt & Pepper to taste

Preheat oven to 350°F.

Sauté chopped onion, sage, and celery in 1 tbsp oil and 1 tbsp butter in a large skillet over medium heat. Once onions are translucent, transfer to medium bowl. Add Applejack and the sage and remaining butter, and then chopped fruitcake to mixture and toss. Bake about 30 minutes.

Crunchy Asian Noodle Salad

Kosher salt
½ lb. thin spaghetti
1 lb. sugar snap peas
1 cup vegetable oil
¼ cup rice wine vinegar
1/3 cup soy sauce
3 tbsp dark sesame oil
1 tbsp honey
2 garlic cloves, minced
1 tsp grated fresh ginger
3 tbsp toasted white sesame seeds, divided
½ cup smooth peanut butter
2 red peppers, cored, seeded, thinly sliced
4 scallions (white and green parts), sliced
3 tbsp chopped fresh parsley leaves

Cook the spaghetti al dente. Drain and set aside. Meanwhile, bring a large pot of salted water to a boil, add snap peas, return to a boil, and cook for 3-4 minutes, until crisp tender. Lift snap peas from the water with a slotted spoon and immerse in a bowl of ice water. Drain. **For the dressing**, whisk together the vegetable oil, rice wine vinegar, soy sauce, sesame oil, honey, garlic, ginger, 2 tbsp sesame seeds and peanut butter in a medium bowl. Combine spaghetti, snap peas, peppers and scallions in a large bowl. Pour the dressing over and add the remaining 1 tbsp of sesame seeds and parsley and toss.

Roasted Baby Beets

with Gorgonzola & Walnut Dressing

2 lbs. baby beets, trimmed (if not using baby beets, halve or quarter the beets)
2 tbsp olive oil
½ tsp coarse salt
¼ tsp black pepper.

Dressing
2 tbsp extra-virgin olive oil
¼ cup chopped walnuts
¼ red onion, thinly sliced
1 tbsp balsamic vinegar
¼ tsp coarse salt
3 ounces Gorgonzola cheese
¼ cup light or heavy cream

Preheat oven to 425 °.

Roast the beets, with 1 tbsp olive oil, 1/4 tsp salt and 1/8 tsp pepper in a roasting pan and cook until the beets are tender, about 40 minutes. When they are cool enough to handle, remove the skins and slice the beets.

Place the beets in a medium-sized mixing bowl and toss with the remaining 1 tbsp olive oil, 1/4 tsp salt, and 1/8 tsp pepper.

Dressing: Place a large skillet over medium-high heat and, when it is hot, add the extra-virgin olive oil. Add the walnuts and cook until they are browned, about 2 to 3 minutes.

Transfer to a small mixing bowl and when the walnuts have cooled to room temperature, add the onion, vinegar and salt.

Place the Gorgonzola cheese and cream in a blender or food processor fitted with a steel blade and process until smooth. Transfer to the bowl with the walnuts and mix to combine.

Serve immediately with a large dollop of the dressing. Serves 4 to 6

Sweet & Spicy Eggplant

3 medium eggplants (about 2 lbs.)
4 tbsp olive oil
4 garlic cloves, crushed in a pestle
3 tbsp honey
4 tbsp lemon juice
1 small spoonful harissa or ¼ tsp cayenne
1 tsp cumin
1 tsp finely-minced fresh ginger
salt to taste

Peel the eggplants, and cut into 1/4 inch thick slices. Brush both sides of the slices with olive oil.

Heat a large non-stick frying pan over medium high-heat. Fry eggplant, turning once, until golden brown. Set aside.

Remove pan from the heat, and allow to cool for a minute or two. Add olive oil and garlic, and leave the garlic to soften. When the aroma of the garlic has been released, add the honey, lemon juice, harissa, spices and salt to taste. Stir to blend.

Return the eggplant to the pan, and bring the sauce to a simmer over medium heat. Cook the eggplant for about 10 minutes, or until the eggplant is tender and the sauce has a syrup-like consistency. Add a little water during the cooking if you feel it's necessary, but not so much that the eggplant will overcook while the liquids reduce. Serves 4 to 6 as a side.

Haricot Casserole

Loubia b'Zeit

1 ¼ lb fresh green beans
1 ¼ lb ripe tomatoes, peeled & chopped
1 large onion, finely chopped 8 unpeeled
cloves of garlic
5 tbsp olive oil
salt to taste

Top, tail and de-string the green beans, and
chop them into 2" pieces. Heat the olive oil
in a pan over a medium heat. Add the
chopped onions and garlic and sauté until
they turn golden, about 10 minutes. Add
the beans, sprinkle with a generous pinch
of salt and sauté for a few minutes, or till
the beans turn glossy and bright green.

Pour in the tomatoes, add salt to taste, mix
well and cover the pan. Simmer gently for
about 40 minutes or until the sauce has
thickened and the beans are done to your
liking. Serve warm (it is also delicious cold)
with warmed pita bread. Serves 4-6.

Easy Fig & Sage Risotto

This recipe does not follow the traditional risotto method: the rice is stirred for a few minutes toward the end of cooking instead of constantly throughout. The consistency is largely a matter of personal taste; if you prefer a looser texture, add extra broth.

6 ½ cups vegetable stock
4 tbsp unsalted butter
1 large onion, chopped fine (1 ½ cups)
1 tsp salt or to taste
2 medium garlic cloves, minced
2 cups Arborio rice
1 cup dry white wine
1 ½ cups (9 ounces) Calmyrna Figs,
        stemmed and cut into ¼" pieces
1 ½ cups freshly grated Parmesan
1 tbsp chopped fresh parsley
3 tbsp chopped fresh sage
Freshly-ground black pepper

Bring stock to a boil in large saucepan over high heat. Reduce heat to medium-low to maintain a gentle simmer.

Heat 2 tbsp butter in a large Dutch oven over medium heat. When butter has melted, add onion and ¾ tsp salt. Cook, stirring frequently, until onion is softened but not browned, 5 or 6 minutes. Add garlic and stir until fragrant, about 30 seconds. Add rice and cook, stirring frequently, until grains are translucent around edges, 3 minutes.

Add wine and cook, stirring constantly, until fully absorbed, 2 to 3 minutes. Stir 5 cups hot stock into rice; reduce heat to medium-low, cover, and simmer until most of the liquid is absorbed and rice is just al dente, about 20 minutes, stirring a couple of times.

Add ¾ cup hot broth mixture and stir gently and constantly until risotto becomes creamy, about 3 minutes. Stir in diced figs and Parmesan. Remove pot from heat, cover, and let stand 5 minutes. Stir in remaining 2 tbsp butter, parsley and sage. Season with salt and pepper to taste. If desired, add up to 3/4 cup remaining broth mixture to loosen texture of risotto. Serve immediately.

Makes 6 servings

Rice & Chick Peas, Fatté

3 cups dry chickpeas
1 tsp baking soda
5 ¼ cups water
3 sticks cinnamon
1 tbsp coarse sea salt
4 loaves toasted pitas
3 tbsp unsalted butter
1/3 cup pine nuts
2 cloves garlic, crushed
½ oz mint leaves
4 cup plain yogurt

The night before, put the chick peas in 3 times their volume of water to soak, and stir in the baking soda. They will double in size & soften. If you must you can use good canned chick peas.

The next day, rinse the chickpeas in cold water, put them in a saucepan, cover with fresh water and place over medium heat. Bring to the boil and cook for 1 hour or until they are done.

Toast the bread in a hot oven or grill until golden brown in color and leave to cool.

Melt butter in a frying pan and sauté pine nuts, stirring regularly or until golden brown. Remove with a slotted spoon onto a double layer of paper towels and drain.

Mix the crushed garlic and the mint into the yogurt; add salt to taste, and set aside.

Break the toasted bread into bite-sized pieces and spread over the bottom of a deep serving dish. Place the rice on top of this. Drain chickpeas and spread over the rice. Top with the yogurt and sprinkle pine nuts on top.

This versatile dish can be served as a vegetarian offering or you can serve with beef, lamb or chicken.

Moroccan Couscous

Here is Paula Wolfert's foolproof method of preparing precooked couscous. You need the same volume of salted water as couscous, and allow 1 pound for 4 people.

Put 2 ½ cups couscous in an oven dish. Gradually add 2 ½ cups warm salted water (made with about ¾ tsp salt,) stirring vigorously so that water is absorbed evenly. Leave to swell for 10 minutes.

Mix in 2 tbsp excellent extra-virgin olive oil, and rub the couscous between your hands to air it and break up any lumps.

Put the dish in an oven preheated to 400°F and heat through for 20 minutes or until it is steaming hot.

Before serving, work in 3 tbsp butter cut into small pieces (or 3 tbsp of very good olive oil) breaking any lumps and let it fluff up again before serving.

Harissa Sauce

1 oz dried red chili peppers
2 cloves garlic
2 tsp ground caraway
salt to taste
extra-virgin olive oil
mortar and pestle

Cover peppers with hot water and soak for an hour. Drain and cut into small pieces. Place in mortar and lb. into a puree with the garlic and spices. Sprinkle with a little salt.

To preserve, spoon into a jar with a tight-fitting lid, cover with a layer of olive oil. Seal tightly and refrigerate.

Vegetable Couscous

¼ cup cooking oil
1 large onion, cut into thin slices
4 carrots, cut into thin slices
1 fennel bulb, cored, cut into 1-inch pieces
1 medium eggplant cut into 1/2-inch pieces
4 cloves garlic, minced
1 jalapeño pepper, including seeds and ribs, cut diagonally into thin slices
1/4 cup tomato paste
2 tsp ground coriander
1 ½ tsp caraway seeds
2 ¼ tsp salt
¼ tsp fresh-ground black pepper
5 ½ cups water
15 oz drained, rinsed chickpeas

1 1/3 cups couscous

In a large saucepan, heat the oil over moderate heat. Add the onion, carrots, fennel, eggplant, garlic, and jalapeño.

Cook, covered, until the vegetables start to soften, about 10 minutes. Stir in the tomato paste, coriander, caraway seeds, 2 tsp of the salt, and the black pepper. Cook, stirring, for about a minute.

Add 3 1/2 cups of the water and bring to a boil. Reduce the heat and simmer, uncovered, until the vegetables are tender, about 15 minutes. Add the chickpeas and simmer 2 minutes longer.

Meanwhile, in a medium saucepan, bring the remaining 2 cups of water to a boil. Add the remaining 1/4 tsp salt and the couscous. Cover. Remove the pot from the heat and let the couscous stand for 5 minutes. Fluff with a fork.

Serve on top or next to the couscous as a vegetarian dish or side. If serving with a Tagine or stew, pour it with its broth over the couscous.

Jeweled Rice with Dried Fruits

This is one of the glories of Persian cuisine and a favorite at wedding banquets, where it is meant to bring good luck and sweetness to the happy couple. Despite its sumptuous, exotic appearance, it is not that difficult to make.

Here's a somewhat simplified version.

3 cups white basmati rice
3 tbsp salt
½ cup dried apricots, quartered
½ cup golden raisins
½ cup dried cherries
8 tbsp unsalted butter
½ tsp ground cardamom
½ tsp freshly ground black pepper
½ cup coarsely chopped pistachios

Wash rice in several changes of cold water in a large bowl until water is almost clear. Let drain in a large sieve for several minutes. Bring 4 quarts water and salt to a boil in a 6-quart heavy pot. Add rice and boil, uncovered, stirring occasionally.

Once the rice has absorbed all the liquid, but is still tender, remove rice to a bowl.

Layer dried fruits and rice alternately in pot, beginning and ending with rice and mounding it loosely.

Make 5 or 6 holes in rice to bottom of pot with handle of a wooden spoon. Cover pot with a kitchen towel and a heavy lid and fold edges of towel up over lid, so the towel won't burn.

Cook over moderately low heat until rice is tender and crust has formed on bottom, 30 to 35 minutes. Remove from heat and let stand, tightly covered for at least 30 minutes.

Melt remaining 2 tbsp butter in a small skillet let over moderate heat. Add pistachios and cook, stirring, until toasted, about 2 minutes. Remove from heat.

Spoon loose rice onto a platter. Dip bottom of pot in a large bowl of cold water for 30 seconds to loosen the crust. Remove crust with a large spoon and serve over rice. Sprinkle with pistachios.

Serves 8.

Angel Hair Pasta with Garlic & Olive Oil

Deceptive in its simplicity, this delicious Italian side requires very careful attention because it is made so quickly. Use your very best extra-virgin olive oil and local hard-neck garlic.

8 garlic cloves, peeled, thinly sliced
3 tsp. fresh parsley, chopped
½ cup extra-virgin olive oil
1 lb angel hair pasta (cappellini d'Angelo)
Salt & freshly-ground pepper to taste
Fine unseasoned bread crumbs (home-made if you can)

Carefully following, the directions on the pasta packaging, cook pasta *al dente*. Immediately remove from water and rinse with cold water to stop the cooking. Drain well and set aside.

In a skillet, sauté garlic, parsley salt and pepper quickly over medium heat. When the garlic just begins to turn golden remove from heat immediately.

Toss pasta in the pan to coat evenly. Serve with a sprinkling of bread crumbs.

Entrées

Skillet-Roasted Split Chicken

Preheat oven to 450°F. Using kitchen shears or a sharp knife, cut alongside the backbone of the chicken to split it open. Spread and press on the chicken with your hands to flatten it. Using a sharp paring knife, cut halfway through both sides of the joints connecting the thighs and drumsticks and cut through the joints of the shoulder under the wings as well. This will help the heat penetrate these joints and accelerate the cooking process.

Put the chicken skin side down on a cutting board and rub with lemon halves all over then salt and pepper generously.

Cook over high heat about 5 minutes, then place the skillet in the oven and cook the chicken for about 30 minutes. It should be well browned and dark on top. Let it rest in skillet at room temperature before serving.

Crispy Duck Leg Confit

4 Duck Legs Confit
4-5 tbsp Vegetable Oil to cover a skillet
4 tbsp Hoisin sauce
4 scallions
1-2 tbsp Rice wine vinegar
4 portions of organic baby greens

Very quickly cook off the Confit in a large skillet covered with vegetable oil on high heat, bottom sides first, then fat sides until crispy. Be sure to cook it hot enough so the legs sear quickly and do not absorb any of the oil. Remove from skillet and let all excess oil drain off.

Clean the scallions using only the bottom two-thirds and slice very finely.

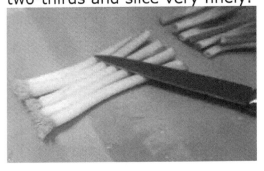

Mix the hoisin with a whisk adding the rice wine vinegar a little at a time so the mixture is thick and not runny, and then add the sliced scallions.

Place a leg on a bed of baby greens, and serve with the sauce on the side.

Making Duck Legs Confit

4 Duck Legs with thigh
8 Garlic Cloves
4 Bay Leaves
1 tsp Peppercorns
3-4 sprigs each of fresh Thyme and Sage
2 tbsp of Sel Gris (or Kosher salt)
2-3 cups rendered Duck Fat and/or Olive Oil
(enough to cover legs)

The day before.

Some recipes suggest you poke tiny holes
throughout duck skin being very careful not
to pierce the meat. **Don't do it!** In fact
look for smooth, unblemished skin.

Rub the duck legs with the smashed garlic
cloves and then salt them generously. Tear
the bay leaves and thyme sprigs and add
the peppercorns and roll the legs so they
are evenly covered. Add a couple of

tablespoons of the olive oil to the baking pan (the smaller the better, so it just fits the legs,) and arrange the legs fat side up.

You can tightly cover and refrigerate for a day or 2. Bring to room temperature when ready, remove the legs and gently rub off all the covering and reserve.

Very lightly cover the bottom of a cast-iron skillet or Le Creuset with olive oil over medium heat and very quickly sear the legs, first the bottom side, and then the fat side. Return to the baking pan fat side up and barely cover with olive oil, rendered duck fat or a combination. The duck skins should be just above the liquid. Sprinkle seasonings back on top to cover evenly.

Place in a 250°F oven for 2-3 hours or until very tender to the touch. Remove all the liquid and reserve. You can prepare immediately, or you pack carefully in a crock or a heavy-duty food-safe plastic freezer bag when cool. Pour liquid over and either refrigerate or freeze.

Grilled Oriental-marinated Flank Steak

Flank steak (or London Broil) is delectable and tender if you make it this way.

3-4 lb. flank steak
1/3 cup olive oil
6 cloves garlic, smashed
2 Tbsp rice wine vinegar
1 cup soy sauce
1/3 cup mild honey or corn syrup
fresh ginger root

At least 3 hours or the night before combine the marinade ingredients. Coat the steak well with the marinade in a large flat Pyrex dish so it is completely covered. Cover with Saran wrap and refrigerate.

Take out about ½ hour before cooking to bring to room temperature.

Preheat your grill to high heat.

Take the steak out and remove any garlic or ginger stuck to it. Grill for 4-6 minutes to sear (until it lifts easily off the grill.) If you are using a gas grill, cover the grill. Turn over and grill about 5-6 minutes. Finish the first side now by turning the steak 90° so that you get more grill marks.

The best way you know if the steak is done to tell is to poke it with your fingertips. While the steak is still raw, it will be quite squishy. Flank steak is best eaten medium rare; well-done will make it too tough.

When the steak has cooked to your preferred level of doneness, remove from the grill and place on a cutting board. Let rest for 10 minutes. Make very thin slices, against the grain, and at a slight diagonal. Serve with softly-caramelized onions & Gorgonzola cheese

Magret de Canard

A true magret de canard is the breast meat of a force-fed duck raised to produce foie gras. The breasts are extremely thick and have a much beefier taste than ordinary duck breasts. Like steaks in France, they are served rare. D'Artagnan and other producers in the nearby Hudson Valley offer fabulous examples of this delicacy.

Take two raw duck breasts, trim them of any excess fat and nerve tissue.

Using a sharp knife, score the layer of fat on the top of the magret de canard diagonally, making cuts spaced about an inch apart. You want to cut about halfway through the fat, not all the way down to the meat. Then, score in the other direction, making a cross-hatched pattern in the fat. This will help the fat contract evenly when you sear the breast.

This isn't just for decorative effect: it's about the fat. You can certainly do without this step and just cook like a steak, but be careful to cook the fat through. Rub both sides with salt and freshly ground pepper.

Heat a large frying pan till it's smoking hot. Don't bother with any cooking oil, because the fat released from the skin will be more than sufficient to cook the breasts.

Place the breasts in the pan, skin side down. Cook for 3-4 minutes until the skin is browned and crisp.

Add about 15 green peppercorns and 20 pink peppercorns, whole or crushed.

Turn the breasts over and cook for about 5-6 minutes for rare, or slightly longer if you prefer them medium.

Pour off all the excess fat from the pan and add a good slug of cognac. Carefully light it with a match (or be a fancy-pants chef, tip the pan slightly and ignite it on the gas flame) and remove the breasts either when the flames have died away.

Set the duck aside, cover it with baking foil to keep warm and let it rest well. Meanwhile deglaze the pan to make the particular sauce that you fancy.

To "deglaze" (déglacer) a pan means stirring away at the bottom of it, giving it a good scrape so that you "liberate" all those yummy cooked particles, getting them to dissolve into the gravy.

One of the simplest duck sauces is Marsala. Heat the juices left in the pan after you've poured off the fat, pour about a wine glass of Marsala into the pan over a moderately high heat, and deglaze the pan.

Instead of Marsala, you could deglaze the pan with about a third of a pint of stock over a medium heat until the liquid is reduced by half.

Then take the pan off the heat and add a large knob of softened butter little by. Whisk the butter in, shifting the pan back onto the heat occasionally so that the sauce thickens and emulsifies.

Pan-fried Meatloaf

Make the meatloaf ahead of time. Bring to room temperature and fry thick slices in butter for a delicious twist on an American favorite comfort food!

Cold Meatloaf (see next recipe)
3-4 tbsp unsalted butter

Bring meatloaf to room temperature. Slice into 1½" or thicker slices.

When the butter is sizzling in the skillet, place the meatloaf slices and cook about 3-4 minutes on a side until crispy on the sides and warmed through.

Epicurean All-American Meatloaf

1½ cups coarse fresh bread crumbs
½ cup cream
2 tbsp Worcestershire sauce
4 tbsp Heinz Ketchup
2 tbsp Dijon mustard
2 tbsp Gulden's Spicy Brown Mustard
¼ lb Applewood-smoked bacon, chopped
1½ lbs. ground sirloin
1½ lbs. ground pork (not lean)
1½ lbs. ground veal
3 large eggs

Make sure ingredients are all at room temperature.

Combine the meats, bacon and cream well by hand. Then mix the mustards, ketchup and Worcestershire sauce in a bowl and add to the meat working in thoroughly.

Add the bread crumbs a third at a time with an egg each time, and again work it thoroughly with your hands so it is completely combined.

Form into a loaf, baste with a little ketchup if you wish – you can also drape some nice bacon strips over in a criss-cross pattern. Bake at 350°F about an hour or until a meat thermometer inserted in the center reads 160°F.

Soy-ginger grilled Salmon

2 salmon steaks
2 tbsp olive oil
1 tsp freshly grated ginger
1 tsp minced garlic
2 tbsp soy sauce
2 tbsp olive oil (for grill surface)

Combine marinade ingredients

Cover salmon with marinade and let stand at room temperature for 20 minutes. Flip salmon over after 10 minutes to marinade the salmon equally.

Cook on uncovered grill, directly over heat for 5-7 minutes each side. Baste with remaining marinade while grilling.

Jumbo Lump Crab Cakes

1 large egg
2 heaping tbsp Hellmann's mayonnaise
1 tsp Dijon mustard
1/2 tsp Worcestershire sauce
1/4 tsp Tabasco sauce
Few drops of lemon juice (1/4 tsp)
2 tsp Old Bay Seasoning
1/4 tsp each salt & black pepper
1/2 cup crushed unsalted crackers
2 tbsp chopped fresh parsley
1 lb. fresh jumbo lump crabmeat -- drained
of all excess liquid
chopped yellow & red bell peppers
1 small onion, diced
2 stalks celery, diced
2 tbsp champagne vinegar
dash of extra-virgin olive oil

In a medium bowl, combine the egg,
mayonnaise, mustard, Worcestershire,
Tabasco, lemon juice, Old Bay, salt and
pepper. Mix so that all the ingredients are
well-incorporated. Add the cracker crumbs
and parsley and mix well.

Gently fold in crabmeat until just combined
(try not to break up lumps of crabmeat).

Using wet hands, shape mixture into 6
patties---8 patties if you like them smaller
(do not pack too firmly; cakes should be as
loose as possible and still hold their shape).

Put the crab cakes on a large platter or cookie sheet as they're shaped. Cover with foil and refrigerate at least 1 hour before cooking.

On a flat-top or shallow skillet heat a little vegetable oil over medium-high heat. When oil is hot, cook crab cakes 4-5 minutes on a side. Do not flip until they have developed a golden crust.

Champagne Remoulade Sauce

Not a classic remoulade (which is puréed,) this sauce has a little crunch and makes a lovely dipping sauce for crab cakes and other seafood.

1/3 cup finely-diced cornichons
1 cup mayonnaise
2-3 tbsp Dijon mustard
2 tbsp Champagne vinegar
Pinch freshly ground black pepper

Whisk together Serve cold or at room temperature.

Tagine of Local Lamb

with Prunes, Almonds and LaKama Spices

LaKama is a spice mixture found only in Northern Morocco, and it is used to flavor soups and tagines. Moroccan food — part Arab and part Berber — is not like Middle Eastern. Its cooking and spice mixtures are unique and change from region to region. I don't know of any other Arab country that has such a rich and varied cuisine. **—Paula Wolfert** (The Slow Mediterranean Kitchen)

For the LaKama Spices Combine spices in a small bowl. Set aside.
1 tbsp ground ginger
1 tbsp finely ground black pepper
1 tbsp ground turmeric
2 tsp ground Ceylon or Mexican cinnamon
1 tsp freshly grated nutmeg

For the tagine
1 lb. (18 to 20) pitted large prunes
3-4 lb lamb shoulder, cut into 2-inch chunks
2 tbsp olive oil
4 large garlic cloves, crushed with 1 tsp salt
1 tbsp LaKama spices
Pinch of saffron
1 tsp ground cinnamon
1 tbsp orange flower water
3 tbsp sugar
1 cup blanched almonds, lightly toasted
1 tbsp sesame seeds

Soak the prunes in warm water. Set aside. Trim lamb of excess fat. In a wide tagine or in a skillet slow-cooker, heat the oil with the garlic, LaKama spices, and saffron. Add meat and stir until the aromas of the spices are released and the meat is nicely coated.

Add 2 cups water (it doesn't have to cover the meat), bring to a boil, then lower the heat, cover, and simmer gently for 2 hours. After about an hour, transfer 1/2 cup of the meat juices to a medium skillet, add the drained prunes, cinnamon, orange flower water, and sugar, and cook slowly until the prunes are lightly caramelized, about 25 minutes.

Remove the skillet from the heat. When the meat is tender remove from the heat. Push the prunes to one side in the skillet; return to medium heat. Working in batches, brown chunks of drained lamb in the syrupy prune juices until glazed on all sides.
Skim all the fat off the meat juices. Return the lamb, add the prunes and reheat. Decorate with almonds and sesame seeds and serve.

Tony & Mitch Cooking Moroccan

Deconstructing Rabbit

The Other
"Other White Meat"

And, no, it doesn't really taste like chicken -
- it's a lot more interesting. Although a
mainstay of European cuisine, chefs here
who dare to have rabbit on the menu often
get flack from appalled diners.
Nevertheless, it's a meat source that has
advantages: it's a lean protein that's low in
cholesterol. If you're a do-it-yourselfer,
rabbits are easy to raise, and they breed
like, you know, rabbits.

Yet many Americans suffer from "Easter
Bunny syndrome" relating to rabbits as
cartoon characters, imaginary friends,
bedtime story heroes, annual purveyors of
sugary treats and, yes, pets. Given their
formidable cute factor—we have trouble
thinking of them as a table offering. So we
have a deplorable lack of awareness and
knowledge about how to cook them.

This class not only deconstructs the myths
about rabbit, but also demonstrated how to
physically deconstruct a rabbit, understand
the different parts and cook them in
different ways.

We used rabbits raised at nearby Black Willow Pond Farm– and that is also where the chicken livers came from.

We featured Black Cat specialties, like our Drunken Blonde Fruitcake made into a not-so-sweet stuffing. And our Fig-Balsamic Drizzle highlighted the liver & bacon flavors (as well as the salad.) We also use a Lebanese favorite to sweeten the Rabbit Confit a tiny bit, and that is Pomegranate Molasses.

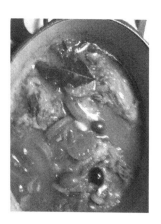 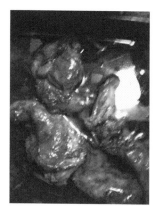

Rabbit Confit

4 rabbit limbs
1 tbsp coarse salt
2 tsp ground black pepper
20 sage leaves; 10 thyme sprigs
8 cloves garlic, crushed and peeled
2 quarts extra virgin olive oil, or as needed.

Toss rabbit, salt, pepper, herbs and garlic in a bowl and refrigerate, covered, for a half-hour or up to 24 hours.

Put rabbit, herbs and garlic in a saucepan just large enough to fit. Cover with olive oil. Turn heat to medium and watch carefully; allow just a few bubbles to come up at a time. Keep oil at 190-200°F and don't allow meat to brown. Cook, turning meat once or twice, for 2 hours or until quite tender but not falling off bone. Remove from oil. You can refrigerate rabbit and oil separately or together, until needed. (If storing separately, use rabbit in a few days; if you store it in oil, it will keep a few weeks.)

When you're ready to cook, put 2 to 4 tbsp of used oil in a skillet large enough to hold rabbit pieces in one layer; set heat at medium-low. (Use leftover oil for other purposes.) Cook the pieces slowly, turning once or twice, until browned and crisp, 10 to 20 minutes. Serve hot, warm or at room temperature, alone or over a bed of greens with a little dressing. 2 to 4 servings.

Provençal Rabbit Stew with Olives

1 whole small rabbit (2 ½ to 3 lbs.)
Extra-virgin Olive oil
Salt and pepper
Flour, for dusting
2 cups leeks, finely sliced
6 garlic cloves, thickly sliced
1 large carrot, finely sliced
1 large sprig thyme
1 medium sprig rosemary
1 bay leaf
1 cup chopped canned whole, peeled
    tomatoes (no juice)
½ cup good dry white wine (whatever you
    plan to drink with the meal)
1 cup unsalted chicken broth.
¾ lb brine-cured green olives

Cut the rabbit into 9 pieces (or ask your butcher to do it) as follows: With a sharp cleaver, cut the saddle (center portion) into 3 pieces, leaving the kidneys attached. Cut the front portion (front legs) in half through the backbone. Chop each hind leg into 2 pieces. Reserve the liver and heart for another purpose.

Heat ¼ inch of olive oil in a Dutch oven or deep, wide heavy skillet over medium heat. Season the rabbit pieces with salt and pepper, then dust lightly with flour. Lightly brown the rabbit for about 3 minutes on both sides, working in batches. Drain on kitchen towels, then transfer to an earthenware baking dish in one layer.

Heat oven to 375°F.

Pour off the used oil, wipe out the pan and add 2 tablespoons fresh oil. Heat to medium-high, add the onions and cook till soft, about 5 minutes. Add the leek, garlic, rosemary and carrots. Season with salt and pepper. Cook for 2 minutes more, stirring.

Add the chopped tomatoes and wine, and let the mixture reduce for 1 minute. Add the broth, bring to a simmer, taste and adjust seasonings.

Ladle the mixture evenly over the rabbit. Cover the dish, and bake for 1 hour. Let rest 10 minutes before serving.

4 servings.

Lebanese Meza

Thyme Flatbread, Man'oosh

2¼ tsp active dry yeast
2 cups all-purpose flour
¾ cup warm water (105-115°F)
1½ tsp salt
1½ tsp olive oil for dough plus 8 tbsp for topping
3 oz Lebanese za'atar spice

The dough can be made a day in advance – let it rise slowly, covered, in the refrigerator. Bring to room temperature before using. (You can also buy pizza dough if you don't have time, but it is not as good.)

Stir together yeast, 1 tbsp flour, and ¼ cup warm water in a measuring cup and let stand until mixture develops creamy foam on surface, about 5 minutes. (If mixture doesn't foam, discard and start over with new yeast.)

Stir together 1 ¼ cups flour with salt in a large bowl. Add yeast mixture, oil, and remaining ½ cup warm water and stir until smooth. Stir in enough flour (about 1/2 cup) to make dough come away from sides of bowl. Knead dough on lightly floured surface with lightly floured hands until smooth, soft, and elastic, about 8 minutes. Form dough into a ball, put on a lightly floured surface, and generously dust with flour. Loosely cover with plastic wrap and let rise in a warm draft-free place until doubled in bulk, about 1¼ hours. Do not punch down dough.

Preheat oven to 450°F.   Carefully dredge dough in a bowl of flour to coat and transfer to a dry work surface. Make 3-4 inch rounds by pinching off a handful of dough and rolling.

Combine the remaining olive oil with the za'atar stirring well to make a smooth paste. Spread thinly on each pizza you form.

Bake for 10 minutes or until cooked through.   Serve with tomatoes and cucumbers to make a delicious hot "wrap"!

Makes 4 large or 12 small flatbreads.

Za'atar

This ancient and ubiquitous Middle Eastern spice is generally prepared using ground dried wild thyme, oregano, marjoram and sumac in varying combinations, mixed with toasted sesame seeds, and salt. This combination varies by country and even by region.

Also delicious on fresh tomatoes drizzled with olive oil, and an excellent garnish for Labneh or Greek Yogurt.

Meat Flatbread, Lahm b'Aajeen

1 onion, finely chopped
1 ½ tomatoes, diced
9 oz lean lamb, ground
1 tsp lemon juice ¼ tsp ground cinnamon
½ tsp ground allspice
2 tbsp pine nuts
salt and pepper to taste

Combine onions and tomatoes in a mixing bowl, season with salt and pepper and mix firmly with hands. Squeeze to drain excess juices. Add meat and remaining ingredients, except pine nuts, and mix well with hands until well-blended.

Let stand for 10-15 minutes. Spread a small amount on each pizza, to cover flatly and thinly. Sprinkle pine nuts on top. Bake in a preheated oven for 10-12 minutes or until bread and nuts are golden brown. Makes 4 large or 12 small flatbreads.

Kibbeh

2 cups Cracked Wheat
2 lbs Ground Lamb or Lean Beef
2 large onions, chopped roughly
2 tsp salt
1 tsp Black Pepper
1 tsp Ground cinnamon

Wash cracked wheat several times in cold water. Allow wheat to stand in water for about 1 hour. Grind meat and onions fine. Mix with seasonings and wheat.

Moisten hands in small bowl filled with cold water. Thorough mixing or kneading of the mixture is very important.

Kibbeh may be fried, grilled over charcoal plain or with a filling. Individual patties are formed into hollow ovals (see picture) or filled.

A very traditional method is to bake with a filling, but he next recipe is a very elegant variation which I prefer.

Kibbeh Topping or Filling

1 lb. onions, sliced
3 tbsp extra virgin olive oil
1/3 cup pine nuts
salt and black pepper
½ tsp ground cinnamon
pinch of ground allspice
1 tbsp pomegranate molasses

Fry the sliced onions in the olive oil until they are golden brown, stirring often. Add the pine nuts and stir until lightly colored. Add a little salt and pepper, cinnamon, and allspice and the pomegranate molasses. Cook, stirring for a minute or so.

This delicious mixture can also be served as part of a meza, or put on top of a dish of Hummus.

Elegant Baked Kibbeh

with Onion and Pine Nut Topping

For Base:
2/3 cup fine-ground bulgur
1 onion, cut in quarters
1 lb. lean lamb
salt and black pepper
1 tsp cinnamon
2 tbsp vegetable oil

For Topping:
Use recipe from previous page.

For the base, rinse the bulgur in a fine sieve under cold running water and drain well. Purée the onion in the food processor. Add the meat, salt, pepper, and cinnamon and blend to a paste. Add the bulgur and blend to a smooth, soft paste.

With your hand, press the paste into the bottom of an oiled, rectangular baking dish. Flatten and smooth the top and rub with 2 tbsp oil. With a pointed knife, cut the contents into 6 or 8 pieces. Bake in an oven preheated to 375°F for about 30 minutes, until browned.

While the base is baking, prepare the topping. Serve the *kibbeh* with the topping spread over the top, cut into approx. 4" squares, with toasted pita bread on the side.

Persian Rice, Lamb, Apricots & Pistachios

2 cups basmati rice
6 tbsp melted butter
1 onion, finely chopped
1 lb. lean lamb, cut into small cubes
½ tsp ground cinnamon
½ tsp allspice
1 cup tart dried apricots, cut in half
3 tbsp golden raisins
1/3 cup shelled unsalted pistachios
salt and pepper

Wash rice in warm water and rinse with cold. Heat 2 tbsp of the butter in a pan and fry onion until golden. Add meat and sauté gently, turning to brown all over. Add spices and half the dried fruits. Top with water and simmer, covered, over low heat for 1½ hours, until meat is very tender. After 1 hour add remaining apricots.

Boil rice in a large heavy-bottomed pan for about 10 minutes. It will be a little underdone. Drain, and mix with 2 tbsp butter. Put remaining butter in the bottom of the pan and mix in a ladle of rice. Arrange alternate layers of rice, meat and apricot sauce, starting and ending with a rice. Cover and steam gently over very low heat for 20-30 minutes, until rice is tender. A cloth stretched under the lid will absorb the steam and make the rice fluffier. Sprinkle with pistachios and serve, scraping up the crunchy rice from the bottom of the pan. Serves 6.

Shrimp in Garlic Sauce

2 lb shrimp, preferably very small, shelled
coarse salt
8 tbsp olive oil
4 cloves garlic, very coarsely chopped
1 dried red chili pepper, seeded, cut in half
½ tsp Spanish paprika
2 tbsp minced parsley

Dry the shrimp well and sprinkle salt on both sides. Let sit at room temperature for 10 minutes. Heat the oil in four ramekins or one shallow 8-inch casserole. Add the garlic and chili pepper, and when the garlic just starts to turn golden (be careful not to overcook) add the shrimp.

Cook over medium-high heat, stirring, for about 2 minutes, or until the shrimp are just done. Sprinkle in the paprika, parsley, and salt.

Serve immediately, right in the cooking dish if possible.

Grilled Lemon Chicken Breast Salad

Marinate the chicken breast in olive oil, crushed garlic, salt and fresh lemon juice for 2-4 hours.

Place on a grill or grill-top on your stove at very high heat and grill about 5-6 minutes a side.

Let rest at least 15 minutes, then slice 4-5 about ½" thick slices on an angle and place on a Mediterranean salad consisting of baby greens, vine-ripened tomatoes, stuffed grape leaves, artichokes, sliced cucumbers with a drizzle of the Lemon Dressing recipe you'll find in this book.

James Beard's Garlic-Studded Lamb Leg

Based on James Beard's method, this makes a delectable roast. Use a local supplier and be sure to get a leg of a baby lamb with the bone in, no more than 5-6 lbs.

Peel and sliver 6-7 cloves garlic. Make small incisions in the fat on the top part of the leg with a very sharp pointed knife. Force the slivers into the incisions. Rub the leg well with salt and freshly-ground pepper* and then place on a rack in a roasting pan.

Roast in a 325°F. oven about 2 ½ hours (a rule of thumb is about 20 minutes a pound) until a meat thermometer shows about 145°F for a rare leg of lamb, in my opinion a tastier, more tender dish (it also leaves lovely leftovers for other dishes.) For well-done, roast to 165°F . Remove and let it stand 20 minutes before carving. The meat will continue to cook during that time.

*Variation: Also rub the leg with grainy mustard mixed with a little olive oil. This will make a gorgeous crust.

Serves 6-8.

Leftover Lamb Shawarma

My favorite thing to do with the leftovers. Lebanese Shawarma is like Greek gyros.

1 tbsp cumin
1 tbsp ground coriander
2 cloves crushed garlic
½ tbsp paprika
1 tsp turmeric
1 tsp ground black pepper
½ tsp ground cinnamon

With a very sharp knife, remove all the meat (esp. from the bone,) and slice into thin strips. Trim fat and in a skillet, fry in a little olive oil, then discard. Toss meat with spices and add to pan. Cook over medium heat until nicely browned but not crisp.

Warm some small pita breads, open and spread with Tahini sauce (or Hummus) add meat, greens, grilled tomatoes, and pickles.

Tahini Sauce

1/2 cup tahini (sesame seed paste)
3 gloves garlic, crushed
1/2 teaspoon kosher salt
¼ cup olive oil
1/3 cup lemon juice
¼ cup warm water

Blend together until smooth & creamy. Can be made ahead and refrigerated. Bring to room temperature before using.

Kafta, Lebanese Ground Lamb

Unlike Kibbeh, Kafta is ground lamb extended with parsley instead of cracked wheat.

2 medium onions, peeled and quartered
1¼ lb. lean minced ground lamb
½ tsp ground cinnamon
½ tsp ground allspice
½ bunch parsley (7 oz), washed, dried and stemmed
¼ tsp finely ground black pepper
Salt to taste

Place the quartered onions and parsley in a blender or food processor and process until finely chopped. Transfer to a mixing bowl and mix the minced meat with the seasonings until you have a smooth paste.

Mix the meat with the parsley and onion by hand until well blended together. Use a small bowl of iced water to dip your hands in while you do this.

Fry in small round ovals, or form on skewers and cook on a grill, preferably over hot charcoal.

Makes about 6 servings.

Serve wrapped in warm pita breads.

Desserts

Sebastian's Flourless Chocolate Cake

My eldest son Sebastian's favorite cake, it is very dense and rich because in addition to the structure the eggs give, it substitutes cocoa powder for the flour. The little secret is that it is also one of the easiest of all cakes to put together.

9 oz good bittersweet chocolate (not unsweetened), chopped, (like Callebaut)
½ lbs. unsalted butter
1½ cups sugar
½ tsp salt
6 large eggs
1 cup unsweetened cocoa powder
10-inch spring-form pan

Put a rack in middle of preheated 350°F oven. Butter pan, line bottom with a round of parchment paper, and butter paper too.

Melt chocolate & butter in a metal bowl set over a pan of barely simmering water. Stir until smooth. Remove bowl and whisk in sugar. Add eggs 1 at a time, whisking well each time. Sift cocoa powder over and whisk until just combined, then add salt.

Pour batter into pan. Bake until top has formed a thin crust and wooden pick inserted in center comes out with moist crumbs adhering, 35-40 minutes. Cool in pan on a rack 10 minutes, then remove side of pan. Invert cake onto a plate and re-invert onto rack to cool completely. Dust cake with cocoa powder before serving.

Caroline's Raisin Bread Pudding

We use a lot of our Raisin Bread for sandwiches and toast at the Café – but what to do with the ends and small pieces? Caroline came up with this lovely solution.

2 cups milk
1 cup heavy cream
3 tbsp butter
1 tsp pure vanilla extract
1 tsp ground cinnamon
1/2 cup raisins
3/4 cup packed brown sugar
3 tbsp Amaretto
8 cups Black Cat's Raisin Bread, cubed
4 eggs beaten

Preheat oven to 350°F.

In a saucepan, heat milk, butter, vanilla, cinnamon & sugar until warm and sugar is all melted. Place cubed bread in a large bowl and add the heated mixture. Let sit for 30 min. or until bread absorbs mixture.

Add the beaten eggs and Amaretto to the bread mixture and stir. Pour into buttered 1½ quart baking dish.

Bake 50 min or until knife inserted comes out clean. Serve hot or cold with warm Amaretto Sauce (see next recipe.)

Amaretto Sauce

2 cups heavy cream
1/2 cup milk
1/2 cup white sugar
2 Tbsp cornstarch
3/4 cup Amaretto
Pinch of salt
2 tbsp unsalted butter

Over medium heat combine the cream, milk and sugar.

Place the cornstarch and 1/4 cup of the Amaretto and whisk to make a slurry. Pour into the cream mixture and bring to a boil.

Once the mixture begins to boil bring to a gentle simmer and cook for 5 minutes stirring occasionally.

Remove from heat add the salt and whisk in remaining 1/2 cup of Amaretto.

Espresso Gelato on Mocha Lava

Place a scoop of a good espresso gelato (we like Ciao Bella) on one of Black Cat's best-loved cookies, and gild the lily with Dark Chocolate Drizzle (next page.)

Mocha Lava Cookies

4 oz unsweetened chocolate
3 cups chocolate chips
1 stick butter
½ cup flour
½ tsp baking powder
½ tsp salt
4 eggs
1 ½ cups sugar
1½ tbsp espresso powder
2 tsp vanilla extract

Preheat the oven to 350°F. Line a cookie sheet with parchment paper. Melt the unsweetened chocolate and 1 ½ cups chocolate chips with the butter.

In the bowl of an electric mixer fitted with a whisk beat the eggs, sugar, espresso powder, and vanilla extract.
Fold the melted chocolate into the eggs and mix until combined.

Mix together the flour, baking powder, and salt. Fold the four mixture and the rest of the chocolate chips into the chocolate and egg mixture.

Let the dough chill for at least 15 minutes. Scoop the dough onto the cookie sheet and bake 8-10 minutes until the cookies are puffed and slightly cracked on top.

Dark Chocolate Drizzle

Melt 2 ounces chopped semisweet or bittersweet chocolate in double boiler over simmering water, stirring often. (Or melt in small microwave-safe bowl in microwave oven on 50% power for 2 to 3 minutes or until smooth, stirring every 30 seconds.) Drizzle over desserts while drizzle is warm.

We love Callebaut for this recipe ...

Wild Strawberries with Fig-Balsamic

Just perfect that simply, or add a scoop of Vanilla Gelato.

Tahitian Vanilla Gelato with Fig-Balsamic Drizzle

Pistachio-Fig Macaroons

1 cup Calmyrna Figs
1 ½ cups raw, unsalted shelled pistachios
¾ cup plus 2 tbsp granulated sugar
1 large egg white
¼ tsp vanilla extract
Chocolate Drizzle recipe, pg. 138

Adjust oven rack to middle position and preheat oven to 325°F.

Remove stems and finely chop figs; set aside. Finely chop 1/2 cup nuts; set aside.

In bowl of food processor, combine remaining 1 cup nuts and sugar. Process until nuts are finely ground. Add egg white and vanilla. Process until dough forms a ball.

Remove dough from processor to separate bowl (dough will be a little sticky). With lightly oiled hands, mix in figs. Form dough into 20 one-inch balls. Roll balls in chopped nuts. Place on large greased baking sheet. Flatten balls to 1 1/2-inch rounds. Bake 15 to 18 minutes, until edges and bottoms are light golden brown; do not over-bake.

Cool on sheet 5 minutes. Remove from wire rack to cool completely. Top with chocolate drizzle, if desired. Makes 20 cookies.

Apple Crostata

1 cup all-purpose flour
2 tbsp granulated sugar
½ tsp kosher salt
¼ lb. (1 stick) very cold unsalted butter, diced
2 tbsp ice water

Make the pastry first. Place flour, sugar, and salt in the bowl of a food processor fitted with a steel blade. Pulse a few times to combine. Add the butter and pulse 12 to 15 times, or until the butter is the size of peas. With the motor running, add the ice water all at once through the feed tube. Keep hitting the pulse button to combine, but stop the machine just before the dough becomes a solid mass. Turn the dough onto a well-floured board and form into a disk. Wrap with plastic and refrigerate for at least 1 hour. Preheat the oven to 450 F.

1½ lbs. Honey Crisp apples, peeled
1 tsp grated orange zest
¼ cup flour
¼ cup granulated sugar
½ tsp kosher salt
½ tsp ground cinnamon
4 tbsp cold unsalted butter, diced

Filling: Peel, core, and cut the apples into eighths. Cut each wedge into 3 chunks. Toss the chunks with the orange zest. Flour a rolling pin and roll the pastry into an 11-inch circle on a lightly floured surface. Transfer it to a baking sheet. Cover the tart dough with the apple chunks leaving a 1½ -inch border.

Combine flour, sugar, salt, cinnamon, and allspice in the bowl of a food processor fitted with a steel blade. Add butter and pulse until the mixture is crumbly. Pour into a bowl and rub it with your fingers until it starts holding together. Sprinkle evenly on the apples. Gently fold the border over the apples to enclose the dough, pleating it to make a circle. Bake for 20-25 minutes, until the crust is golden and the apples are tender. Allow to cool. Serve warm or at room temperature. Serves 6-8.

Honey Crisp Apples

This amazing apple has been our favorite for years now. Refreshing and a bit tart, yet sweet and with a lovely finish. Honey Crisps have a signature high water content that makes for an ultra-crisp bite. A hybrid of Macoun and Honey Gold (1991,) they are thin skinned, sweet, with a lovely outer pinkish green hue and cream colored flesh --- many weigh as much as a pound.

Because of its high water content it is not the best for baking everything, but it still works beautifully for salads & many lightly-baked desserts.

Try mini-apple tarlets made with the **Pâte Sucrée Tartlet Shells** on page 38.

Moroccan Candied Tomatoes

5 lb ripe tomatoes
1 pinch saffron
2 tbsp gum Arabic
4-6 cinnamon sticks
1 ¾ cups granulated sugar
4 tbsp peanut oil

First blanch the tomatoes. Let cool then cut them into round slices.

Add the saffron, gum Arabic, cinnamon sticks (be careful not to break them,) sugar and peanut oil.

Bake in the oven at 300°F for 1 hour to 1 1/2 hours until the tomatoes are candied to your liking.

Sweet Almond Milk Couscous

Based on Mark Bittman's The Minimalist: Couscous Shows Its Sweet Side (October 15, 2008)

2 ½ cups almond milk
1/3 cup sugar
Pinch of salt
1 cup couscous
2 tsp grated orange zest
1 tsp ground cardamom
1 tsp rose water
1 cup sliced or chopped almonds
½ cup shelled pistachios
1 cup chopped dried apricots.

Bring almond milk, sugar and salt to boil in a pot. Add couscous, zest, and cardamom; cover and cook for 1 minute, then turn off heat and let sit for 5 minutes.

Fluff couscous with a fork and sprinkle on the rose water. Add nuts and apricots, and gently combine. Serve warm or at room temperature. 4 servings.

Sweet Couscous With Citrus Salad
Make the couscous with mixed citrus zest — a little lemon, orange, lime or grapefruit — and omit nuts, cardamom and rose water. Let cool to room temperature and serve topped with a cup of orange, tangerine or grapefruit segments (or a combination) tossed with 3 tbsp chopped mint leaves.

Moroccan Sliced Oranges

with Cinnamon, Sugar and Orange Flower Water

Sliced oranges get simple yet sophisticated treatment with a generous sprinkling of ground cinnamon, sugar and orange flower water. A sprig of mint leaves can be added as a garnish if desired.

For each person:

1 navel orange
1 tsp orange flower water
granulated sugar
ground cinnamon

Peel the oranges and removed all the white stuff or pith. Slice into rings, about 1/4 inch thick.

Arrange the orange slices on a plate in a pattern and drizzle with the orange flower water. Generously sprinkle the slices with sugar and cinnamon, and serve immediately.

A Note about Desserts

Many of the desserts we served are not included here, as we often raided the Black Cat Café's bakery ... some of the big favorites were Lush Carrot Cake, Cappuccino Torte, Double Chocolate Cake, Ciao Bella sorbets and more.

Oh, and there's nothing like an excellent coffee or tea to accompany dessert from the Café's huge selection of premium teas and coffees and espresso drinks.

Another one of the Dinner Club benefits of being in the cook's kitchen is you have a much larger range of pre-prepared goodies than you'd ever have at home!

Sources and Bibliography

- James Beard, *various*
- Beekman1802 Heirloom Cookbook
- Black Cat's Cooking Class Cookbook
- Mark Bittman, New York Times, *The Minimalist, various*
- Judith Choate
- Craig Claiborne, *The New York Times Cookbook*
- Bernard Clayton, *Soups and Stews*
- Vanessa Daou
- Epicurious.com, *various*
- Foodnetwork.com, *various*
- Ina Garten, *Barefoot Contessa*
- *Gourmet* Magazine, *various issues*
- Anissa Helou , *Lebanese Cuisine*
- Kat Kinsman, *CNN, eatocracy.com*
- Emeril Lagasse, *Food Network*
- Jacques Pépin, *Today's Gourmet*
- Claudia Roden, *various*
- Saveur Magazine, *various issues*
- Martha Stewart Living, *various issues*
- Paula Wolfert, *various*
- Wikipedia, *various*

Photos
We'd have a lot more pictures, but we never thought to take hi-res images – we were having too much fun! Anyway …

Photographs are ©Black Cat Ventures LLC or taken at Black Cat Dinners or public domain.

Made in the USA
Charleston, SC
20 February 2013